Your Earth, Your World
1st Edition

Copyright © 2013 Fruzsina Varga

All rights reserved. No part of this book may be reproduced or transmitted in any form or by any means, electronic or mechanical, including photocopying or recording, or by any information storage and retrieval system, without permission in writing from the author, except in the case of brief quotations embodied in reviews.

Story by Fruzsina Varga
Book Illustrations by Beatrix-Renata Bihari
Edited by Klara Clark
Book design by Fruzsina Varga and Beatrix-Renata Bihari

Library of Congress Control Number: 2013917116

ISBN-13: 978-0615886909
ISBN-10: 0615886906

Your Earth, Your World

Written by

Fruzsina Varga

"Dedicated to All the children of Earth"

It has oceans and seas and mountains up high,
If you want to go 'round the world
Sometimes you must fly.

Our world is called Earth and it's a beautiful planet,
Many treasures it holds like diamonds and granite.

Earth has many mountains, scraping the sky so high
The tallest one even reaches where the airplanes fly.

The deepest oceans still hold many secrets within,
But if you sit ashore patiently you might see a dolphin's fin.

In lush forests, colorful birds are singing in trees,
While blooming flowers catch the summer breeze.

In daytime you see the Sun;

when the Moon rises, it's night...

Millions of stars fill up the sky and shine, oh, so bright!

There are billions of people sharing Mother Earth,
This beautiful planet,
Show grown ups how to take care of her
And not to take her for granted.

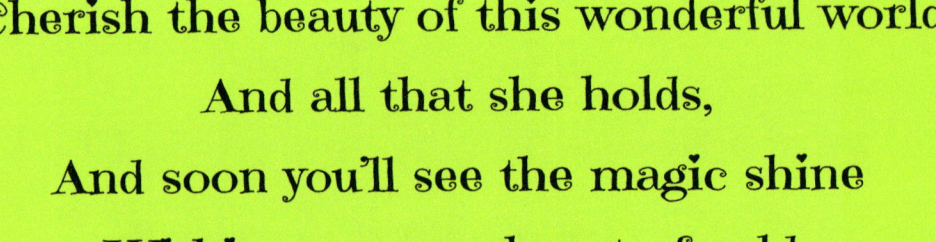

Cherish the beauty of this wonderful world
And all that she holds,
And soon you'll see the magic shine
Within your own heart of gold.

EARTH FRIENDLY FUN ACTIVITIES

The following fun pages are here for you to share your thoughts and put them into action!

1) Do you like drawing or writing?

Now it's your turn! Draw or describe in words, how do YOU see the beautiful Earth? For example do you think animals and people can become friends? Can you write down or illustrate how and in what ways people can take care of the animals?

2) Draw all of your favorite wild animals on these pages!

3) This is a big question but see if you can answer it! Express your thoughts in your own words or images.

What does **PEACE** mean to you?

How do you think you could create peace?

ACTIVITIES with Grown Ups:

1) Find out with the help of your parents or a grown up you trust, how you can volunteer at your local animal shelter! Then write down or illustrate what activities you did!

If you got your picture taken while you volunteered, you can place it in here!

2) Do you want to know what ways you could help nature to stay clean and healthy?

It is just as easy to care for our environment as it is to be careless.

Unfortunately, some people throw trash away and litter on the streets when on a hike or at the beach.

So go on a hike into the nature with your parents or go to the beach and make it very special this time!

Take a trash bag with you and pick up all the trash that you see and place it in the bag and then a designated trash bin.

You will do a great job for the environment and you can also invite your friends to go with you!

How many bags of trash did you collect?

You did a REALLY GREAT JOB and THANK YOU!

Love,

Mother Earth

www.ingramcontent.com/pod-product-compliance
Lightning Source LLC
Chambersburg PA
CBHW042127040426
42450CB00002B/103